Jesus' Important Message

Retold by Lois Rock
Illustrations by Roger Langton

D1270421

K

Jesus had grown up to become a builder and carpenter. But now he spent his time telling people about God.

Grown-ups jostled to talk to him, to ask him important questions. Some of them were rich and clever, with important jobs.

But Jesus wanted everyone to hear what he had to say.

Everyone was important. It didn't matter if they were rich or poor.

And whenever the crowds sat down to listen to him, Jesus always had a special welcome for the children.

What he said often sounded simple.
But it made people think about
important things.

"Imagine that one person tells you to go this way, and another tells you to go that way. Can you obey both of them?

"No, of course you can't.

"Lots of people spend their lives going one way: the way of worrying about money and all the things it can buy.

"I tell you now, that won't make them happy for very long.

"Look at the birds flying round. They don't sow seeds. They don't gather crops. They don't store food in barns.

"But God takes care of them.

"Look at the wild flowers. They don't spin thread. They don't weave cloth. They don't stitch clothes.

"But no one has ever had clothes as beautiful as the petals they wear. God takes care of the flowers.

"I promise you this: God is like the kindest parent ever.

"God really loves you. God will take care of you.

"Who is really happy?

"The people who love the God who loves them, and who set their heart on going the way God wants.

"Who is really happy?

"The people who are kind to others, who forgive their enemies, who settle quarrels.

"Who is really happy?

"The people who follow me and live as God wants. Sometimes they are teased and bullied and hurt for being my friends. But they don't give up.

"At the end of time, God will welcome them, and they will be safe and happy with God for ever."